CANOEING
& OTHER WATER SPORTS

by Jason Page

WATER SPORTS

Grab your life jacket and prepare to set sail as competitors take to the water in the Olympic sailing, rowing and canoeing events!

CANCELLED!

Sailing and rowing events were supposed to have been included in the very first modern Olympics back in 1896. But the weather was so bad that the organizers had to cancel the competitions. As a result, both sports had to wait until 1900 to make their Olympic debut.

SOMETHING OLD

People have been using boats to race on water for thousands of years. One of the earliest examples we know about dates back to 2,500 BCE, when the ancient Egyptians held rowing races on the River Nile.

SUPER STATS

Five countries have attended every single Olympic Games since the competition began in 1896. They are: Australia, Great Britain, France, Greece and Switzerland.

SOMETHING NEW

In a way, sailing made its Olympic debut in Sydney, as it became the first Olympic sport to have a name change. The sport was previously known as yachting. A new sailing event called the 49-er was also introduced at Sydney.

Sailing in a 49-er

OLYMPICS FACT FILE

The Olympic Games were first held in Olympia, in ancient Greece, around 3,000 years ago. They took place every four years until they were abolished in 393 CE.

A Frenchman called Pierre de Coubertin (1863–1937) revived the Games, and the first modern Olympics were held in Athens in 1896.

The modern Games have been held every four years since 1896, except in 1916, 1940 and 1944, due to war. Special 10th-anniversary Games took place in 1906.

The symbol of the Olympic Games is five interlocking coloured rings. Together, they represent the five different continents from which athletes come to compete.

WHAT A RECORD!

The most successful competitor in any water sport was the Danish single-handed yachtsman Paul Elvström. In 1960, he became the first person in Olympic history to win four gold medals in a row in the same event. His Olympic career lasted for 40 years and he attended eight Games from 1948 to 1988 — another record!

Paul Elvström (DAN)

The board is steered by moving the sail using this oval-shaped 'boom' (or 'wish-bone').

The sail is attached to a pole called the 'mast', which swivels, enabling the sail to be turned in any direction.

A small fin, called a 'skeg' on the underside of the board makes it more stable and helps to keep it on course.

All competitors must wear life jackets.

Sailboarding

Foot straps stop the competitor's feet slipping off the board.

DID YOU KNOW?

❦ The RS:X is the only event in which competitors are not penalized for bumping into the buoys.

❦ Sailboarders usually compete barefoot as this improves their grip on the board.

❦ Sailboard competitors use the transparent window in the sail to help them see where they are going.

BUOY OH BOY!

As in other sailing events, competitors in the RS:X have to race around a course marked out using floating markers called 'buoys' (pronounced "boys"). Each race takes about an hour to complete.

MAKING YOUR POINT

Like most Olympic sailing competitions, the RS:X events are decided by a series of 11 'fleet' races, so-called because every competitor takes part in all the races. Competitors are awarded points according to the order in which they cross the finish line — one point for coming first, two for coming second and so on. The winner is the person with the lowest score.

RS:X

Stick a sail on a surfboard and what do you get? The answer is a sailboard — although it goes by many other names!

WHAT'S IN A NAME?

The RS:X is the event previously known as the mistral, so making its Olympic debut at the 2008 Olympics. It is also commonly known as: board sailing, surfboarding, windgliding, sail boarding and windsurfing.

Lee Lai-shan (HKG)

Competitors need strong arms, agility and a superb sense of balance if they want to become a sailboarding champion like Lee Lai-shan (HKG).

SUPER STATS

The greatest speed ever achieved on a sailboard is 91 km/h — that's 10 times quicker than the fastest Olympic swimmer!

Women: Faustine Merret (FRA)

SINGLE-HANDED SAILING

In the single-handed dinghy events, each boat is sailed by one person on their own.

SAILING COURSE

To test the sailors' skills, the Olympic sailing courses are designed so that the wind blows in different directions in different parts of the course.

Here the wind is blowing across the boat from right to left.

Here the boat must sail into the wind using a technique called 'tacking'.

Here the wind is behind the boat.

Here the wind is blowing across the boat from left to right.

STARTING LINE

SUPER STATS

The laser radial is the lightest of all the sailing boats at the Olympics. It weighs around 57 kg, which means it often weighs less than the competitor inside!

TAKE A HIKE

A strong wind can cause a boat to capsize. To prevent this, competitors use a technique called 'hiking out' — they lean out over the water, using their own body weight to balance the force of the wind and keep their boats upright. Here, Ben Ainslie (GBR), the 2004 finn gold medalist, shows us how it's done.

Ben Ainslie (GBR)

WIND

FINISHING LINE

SMALLER AND SMALLER

Sailing made its Olympic debut the 1900 Olympics, and has appeared at every Olympics since 1908 — but the sailing events have changed greatly. The trend in recent years has moved towards using smaller boats with smaller crews. The early Olympic games featured boats with up to 12 crew members. At the 2008 Olympics the largest possible crew can only be made up of three people!

TACKLING TACKING

The hardest part of the course is the stretch which sails into the wind, so here yachtsmen use a technique called 'tacking'. They sail forwards in a zig-zag path, but setting the sails at exactly the right angle and judging when to change course requires great skill.

DID YOU KNOW?

Olympic events involving boats with sails used to be called yachting but the sport was officially renamed sailing at the Sydney Olympics.

Single-handed dinghies are also called 'monotypes'.

At the 1988 Games, Lawrence Lemieux (CAN) was awarded a special medal for rescuing another yachtsman who was swept out to sea after capsizing.

Laser: Robert Scheidt (BRA) / Laser radial: This is a new event and so it was not held at the last Olympics.

Paul Foerster and Kevin Burnham (USA)

This sail is called the mainsail or mainsheet.

TRAPEZE ACT

On a 470, one crew member (the 'helmsman') steers the boat while the other hikes out. By attaching a wire (known as a 'trapeze') to his harness, he is able to lean right out over the water. Above you can see Paul Foerster and Kevin Burnham (USA) the reigning men's champions in action.

The 49-er class dinghies have a double trapeze. This means that both crew members can hike out together and set the sails to catch more of the wind, and so increase their speed.

DID YOU KNOW?

❦ At the Olympics, all the crew members in a boat must be of the same nationality.

❦ The 470 was invented in 1963 and immediately became one of the most popular small sailing boats.

❦ Like most other sailing events, the 49-er class is decided by a series of fleet races; unlike the others, there are 16 races.

THE 407 & 49-ER

In the 470 class, men and women compete in separate events but the 49-er competition is an open event.

49-er with spinnaker

DOUBLE-HANDED DINGHIES

The 49-er is only two Olympics old after making its debut at the 2000 Games.

This sail, called a 'spinnaker', is used for extra speed when the wind is behind the boat.

IN A SPIN

Sailors who break one of the rules of sailing must perform a penalty. This involves sailing around in a circle either once or twice, depending on the boat and the rule broken. If a penalty is not performed properly, sailors risk disqualification.

The small sail in front of the mainsail is called the jib.

ANIMAL OLYMPIANS

With a top speed of around 68 km/h, the 49-er may be the fastest boat at the Games but it's not as fast as the blue-fin tuna, which can travel at 75 km/h.

THE STAR

The star is another double-handed sailing event, but unlike the double-handed dinghy competitions the boats in this category have fixed keels.

STARTER'S SIGNAL

Six minutes before the start of each race, officials in a boat next to the starting line give a signal by firing a cannon or sounding a loud horn. One minute later another signal is given. A third signal is given one minute before the start of the race. The fourth means the race has started.

LEARN THE LINGO

Luff – to sail into the wind

Beat – part of the course that forces the crew to 'luff'

Knot – the speed of boats is often measured in knots: 1 knot equals 1.85 km/h

Inspecting the keel

UNSINKABLE YNGLING

The yngling (pronounced ING-ling) is the women's keelboat event, and their equivalent of the star. It had its Olympic debut in 2004 and will appear in Beijing. The yngling boat has a crew of two or three and is designed to float, even if it is full of water!

Torben Grael and Marcelo Ferreira, Atlanta 1996

The star is an open event. At the 1996 Games it was won by Torben Grael and Marcelo Ferreira (BRA).

KNOW YOUR BOAT

Mast – holds the sails up
Tiller – controls the rudder
Rudder – used to steer the boat
Hull – main body of the boat
Keel – keeps the boat steady
Boom – holds the bottom of the mainsail so that it catches the wind
Bow – the front of a boat
Stern – the back of a boat

The fin on the bottom of a boat is called the keel. It helps the boat to sail in a straight line and keep upright. The keel on a dinghy can be raised or lowered by the crew but the bigger boats in the star class have fixed keels which cannot be adjusted.

DID YOU KNOW?

The first-ever star class boat was built in 1911.

The star event was first held at the Olympics in 1932, but the oldest sailing event at the Games is the finn, which was introduced in 1924.

Between 1948 and 1988, Durward Knowles (GBR/BAH) competed in a record eight Olympic Games.

PROFESSIONAL WEEKENDER

The instantly recognizable laser is one of the most popular single-handed dinghies in the world. It was originally introduced as a recreational boat called the weekender, but it wasn't long before the laser became a favourite in competitive events. The boat made its Olympic debut in 1996.

DID YOU KNOW?

Women have always been allowed to compete against men in the Olympics, but it was not until 1984 that they had their own sailing events.

It is thought that sailing originated in the Netherlands about 400 years ago. The word "yacht" is believed to have come from the Dutch word "jacht" which refers to a small, fast naval boat.

International yacht racing began in 1851 when the New York Yacht Club raced their yacht, named America, around the Isle of Wight in Britain. This competition went on to become the modern day "America's Cup".

Laura Baldwin (GBR)

Robert Scheidt (BRA)

CINGLE-HANDED DINGHIES

There will be three single-handed dinghy events at the Beijing Olympics: the finn, the laser and – making its debut at Beijing – the laser radial.

FINN-TASTIC!

The finn is considered the finest single-handed craft by yachts-people around the world. It is sailed in more countries than any other single-handed boat and has been in every Olympic Games since 1952. To sail a finn, an athlete needs to be physically strong, adept at sailing technique and a clever strategist!

A FAST AND FLEXIBLE FIRST

The laser radial is a small, lightweight boat that will replace the Europe as the women's single-handed event at Beijing. The radial is a lot like the laser – it has a similar hull and uses the same equipment. However, the radial's sail is 19 percent smaller than the laser's, and it has a more flexible lower mast.

SUPER STATS

The USA and Norway have each won 16 gold medals in the sailing events – more than any other nation! Next is Great Britain with 14 medals, and then France with 12.

TORNADO

The event for catamarans at the Olympics is called the tornado – so prepare to be blown away!

COOL CATS

Catamarans have two hulls, one on either side of the deck. They are much lighter than other similar sized boats, enabling them to sail across the water extremely quickly. With a good wind behind them, they can reach a top speed of around 50 km/h.

Gloves help to grip the slippery wet ropes.

Both crew members wear life jackets – just in case they fall overboard!

ANIMAL OLYMPIANS

You wouldn't get far in a catamaran if you were being chased by a hungry tiger shark! These fearsome fish can swim faster than even the fastest catamarans. And if there was a gold medal for eating people they might win that too!

HARBOUR VIEW

The sailing events at the Beijing Games will take place in Qingdao, in China's Shandong province. The competitors will get a good view of the red 'Wind in May' monument, seen here in the centre and the city on the skyline.

Lightweight rubber shoes with ribbed soles stop the yachtsmen slipping.

Some yachtsmen wear a wet suit to help them keep warm, but others don't bother!

Roman Hagara & Hans Peter Steinacher (AUT)

DID YOU KNOW?

🎵 The design of the catamaran is based on an ancient type of boat invented thousands of years ago in Asia.

🎵 The course used in the tornado class is designed so that the race will last about 90 minutes.

🎵 Catamarans aren't the only kind of boat with more than one hull. There's also a three-hull boat called a trimaran.

Qingdao, China

FATHER & DAUGHTER

The great Danish yachtsman Paul Elvström took part in the Olympics for the first time in 1948. His last Olympic race was in 1988 when he sailed in the tornado event. His partner in the race was his daughter, Trine.

SILVER: USA / BRONZE: ARGENTINA

Only six lanes are used in each race.

The water on the course must not be more than 3.5 metres deep.

DID YOU KNOW?

🎗 Rowing events at the Olympic Games used to be held on flowing rivers.

🎗 After winning the men's individual sculls in 1956, Vyacheslav Ivanov (URS) threw his gold medal up into the air – it landed in Lake Wendouree, Australia and was lost forever!

🎗 Even though rowing events are now held on still-water courses, the water and weather conditions still vary too much to allow official world or Olympic records.

The course is divided into nine lanes, separated by coloured buoys.

THE COURSE

Sculling races, like all the other rowing events, are 2,000 metres long and take place on a perfectly straight, man-made course, which is sheltered from the wind. Its banks are sloped and covered in gravel to help absorb waves, keeping the surface of the water flat and still.

SCULLING

NEW ZEALAND

In the sculling events each competitor has two oars, one in each hand.

Katrin Rutschow-Stomporowski (GER)

Katrin Rutschow-Stomporowski won a gold medal in sculls at both the 1996 and 2004 Games.

WINNING QUALITIES

Rowing requires powerful arm, chest, leg and stomach muscles. Maintaining a steady pace with the oars is crucial and requires precise timing which is why top rowers, such as Katrin Rutschow–Stomporowski (GER), also need a superb sense of natural rhythm.

Rowers wear lightweight shorts and vests made out of stretchy materials.

In rowing, boats travel backwards.

The colour of the buoys indicates the distance to the finish line.

WOMEN: Single sculls: Katrin Rutschow-Stomporowski (GER) / **Double sculls:** Georgina Evers-Swindell & Caroline Evers-Swindell (NZL) / **Lightweight double sculls:** Constanta Burcica & Angela Alupei (ROM) / **Quadruple sculls:** GERMANY

SWEEP OAR (CONT'D)

Make way for the mighty 'Eights', the largest — and fastest — rowing boats at the Games.

The cox is the only person in the boat who can see where to go!

WHY 8 = 9!

The Eights are 'sweep oar' rowing events. Unlike sculling races, each rower has only one oar, not two. Eights are so-called because they are rowed by eight people — although there are actually nine people on board each boat! The extra crew member is the 'coxswain' ('cox' for short).

SUPER STATS

The boats used in the Eights are 17 metres long — that's just over twice the length of a single scull boat!

IN THE DRIVING SEAT

The cox's job is to keep the other members of the team rowing in a smooth steady rhythm and to decide how fast they should row. Coxes are also responsible for steering the boat and making it go in a straight line.

GOLDEN BOY

At the Games in 1900 (before minimum weight limits were introduced) one team decided that their cox was too heavy, so they asked a young boy in the crowd to take his place! The team and their new cox won the final and the boy (name unknown and thought to be less than 10 years old) was presented with a gold medal.

Lightweight Eights (GBR)

DID YOU KNOW?

♫ The cox in Olympic races must be the same sex as the rest of the crew.

♫ A crew can continue racing if one of the rowers falls out of the boat but not if the cox falls out!

♫ The youngest cox whose age and name was known for certain was 12-year-old Noel Vandernotte (FRA) who won two gold medals in 1936.

LIGHT WORK

Although a light cox is best, there are minimum weight limits: 55 kg in the men's event and 50 kg in the women's. If the cox weighs less than the limit, extra weight is added to the boat to make up the difference.

The German cox next to one of his team-mates, Barcelona 1992

Drew Ginn & James Tomkins (AUS)

OARSOME!

Drew Ginn & James Tomkins (AUS) celebrate their 2004 win at the Athens Games.

The competitors' shoes are attached to a plate on the bottom of the boat.

The seats inside the boat are mounted on rails to allow the rowers to slide forwards and backwards while they row, and increase the power of each stroke.

SWEEP OAR (COXLESS)

There are four other sweep oar rowing races at the Olympics but there is no room for a cox in these events.

UNDER STARTER'S ORDERS

At the start of each race the boats are held in position by a device called a 'boot'. When the crews are ready, an official shouts 'Two minutes' and reads out the names of all the competitors taking part. If the light controlled by the judges has turned white, he shouts 'Attention!' then presses a button which gives out a loud beep. At the same time the boot automatically releases the boats.

THE EVENTS

The coxless pairs is a race with one event for men and another for women, plus men-only events — the coxless four and the lightweight coxless four.

LEARN THE LINGO

Bow – name also given to the rower who sits at the front

Stroke – name given to the person who sits at the back of the boat

Shell – another name for a racing boat

The boats are usually made of wood.

Rowing boat

The outrigger supports the weight of the oar, helping the boat to go faster.

CANOE

Unlike a rowing boat, the paddle which powers a canoe must not be fixed to the boat in any way.

ANCIENT ORIGINS

Native Americans made canoes from hollowed-out tree trunks which they knelt in to paddle. Modern canoes are based on this design, but are much more streamlined than the traditional-style canoe shown below.

The paddles are not fixed to the boat and are used on either side.

Canadian canoe with oars

Today's canoes still partly resemble hollow tree trunks in shape, but are made of fibreglass.

Canoeists kneel inside the canoe and so there are no seats.

PADDLE POWER

The paddles used by canoeists have a handle to grip on to at one end and a flat blade for pushing through the water at the other. The paddles are also used to steer, as paddling hard on one side makes the canoe turn towards the other side.

SUPER STATS

For many years the former Soviet Union held the record for the canoe and kayak events, with 22 gold medals. But the longstanding record has been beaten by Germany, which now holds 30 gold medals. Hungary has notched up 17 golds.

IT'S A MAN'S WORLD

Sprint races take place over 500 metres and 1,000 metres and there are events for one-man and two-man canoes. However, there are no canoeing events for women.

Martin Doktor (CZE), Atlanta 1996

DOING THE DOUBLE

The sprint events are a simple headlong dash to the finish line. The winner is the first to cross the line — as long as the boat is the right way up! Both the individual sprints at the 1996 Olympics were won by Martin Doktor (CZE).

DID YOU KNOW?

The different canoe events at the Olympics are often given letters and numbers. For example, 'C1' means a one-man canoe race and 'C2' a two-man event.

Canoeists are forbidden to ride on the wash (waves) created by another competitor's canoe in front of them.

Canoes are only allowed to have a tiny keel which mustn't stick out more than 3 cm from the hull.

Canoe double 500: Guanliang Meng & Wenjun Yang (CHN) / **Canoe double 1000:** Christian Gille & Tomasz Wylenzek (GER)

KAYAK

When is a canoe not a canoe? When it's a kayak!

TRADITIONAL DESIGN

Modern kayaks, like canoes, are also based on a traditional type of boat. Kayaks were invented by the Inuit people who live in the Arctic. They would stretch seal skins over frames made out of whalebone and then rub blubber (fat from seals and whales) all over the finished boats to make them watertight.

GOLDEN GIRLS

The women's sprint races are 500-metres long while there are 500-metres and 1,000-metres races for men. As in the canoe events, there are races for both one- and two-person kayaks, known as 'K1' and 'K2' for short.

SPOT THE DIFFERENCE

Competitors in kayaks sit down to paddle, unlike Olympic canoeists who kneel. Another difference is that sprint kayaks have a rudder. The paddles are different too — kayak paddles are longer and have a blade at each end.

Antonio Rossi (ITA)

SPLIT SECOND VICTORY

After the 1,000-metres kayak sprint at the 1988 Games, the judges deliberated for more than 10 minutes before announcing that Greg Barton (USA) had crossed the finish line first — just 0.005 seconds ahead of Grant Davies (AUS)!

Greg Barton (USA)

SUPER STATS

By holding onto each other's paddles, several people join their kayaks together to form a raft. The largest raft ever formed in this way was made up of 648 different kayaks.

DID YOU KNOW?

♙ Between 1948 and 1960, Gert Fredriksson (SWE) won six gold medals, a silver and a bronze in Olympic kayak events.

♙ At the Games in 1936, there were separate events for 'folding' kayaks which could be dismantled and carried around in bags.

♙ Kayaks were introduced into Europe 150 years ago by an English lawyer named John MacGregor.

Antonio Rossi (ITA) won the gold medal at the 1996 Games in the men's K1 500-metres single and K2 1,000-metres races.

KAYAK: FOURS

When travelling at full speed, competitors in the four-person kayak can paddle at up to 130 strokes per minute — that's more than two strokes every second!

PULLING TOGETHER

This picture was taken during the women's fours event at the 1996 Olympics. Look closely and you will see how every member of each team is holding their paddle in almost exactly the same position. In kayak and canoe events, as in rowing, precise rhythm and timing are the key to success.

SUPER STATS

A four-person kayak has a top speed of more than 20 km/h — that's fast enough to pull someone along on water-skis!

Women's kayak fours, Atlanta 1996

Look carefully at the paddle. Notice how the two blades at each end are set at different angles. This means that as one blade is being pulled flat-side-on through the water the other is cutting through the air thin-side-on.

Flat water canoe

CLEAN SWEEP

At the 1996 Games in Atlanta, USA, the men's and women's K4 events were both won by the teams from Germany. It was the first time one nation had won both events at the same Games.

DID YOU KNOW?

The four-person kayak made its Olympic debut in 1964.

Women took part in the event for the first time in 1984.

The men's K4 race is twice as long as the women's event. Men race over 1,000 metres while women compete over 500 metres.

READY, STEADY, GO

Kayak races are started by an official stationed in a small hut alongside the starting line. When all the competitors are ready, the starter shouts 'Attention, please' then fires a starting pistol. A competitor who jumps the gun twice and makes two false starts is disqualified.

NO PENALTIES

Canoeists in the slalom events try to go around the course as quickly as possible, avoiding penalties. A 2-second penalty is added on to the final time if they (or their paddle or canoe) touch one of the gate poles. Missing out a gate incurs a massive 50-second penalty!

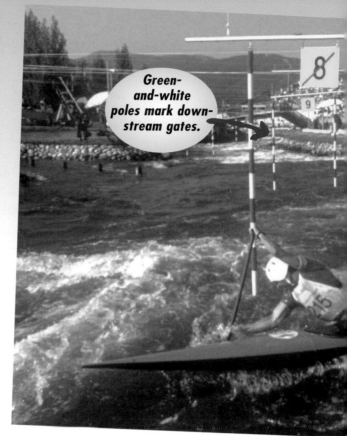

Green-and-white poles mark down-stream gates.

DID YOU KNOW?

🎵 In 1992, 12-times World Champion Jon Lugbill (USA) finished the course in the fastest time but missed out on a medal because his life jacket just touched a pole on the gate second from last!

🎵 Competitors start the course at 180-second intervals.

🎵 Slalom events in canoes, like the sprint events, are a men-only competition.

Michal Martikan (SVK) was only 17 years old when he won the gold medal in the individual slalom event at the 1996 Games.

Michal Martikan, Men's C1 slalom, Atlanta 1996

SLALOM CANOES

The boats used in slalom events are wider and shorter than the ones used in sprint races, and the top of a slalom canoe is covered over to prevent water coming in over the sides. Canoeists paddle kneeling down using a paddle with only one blade.

CANOE: SLALOM

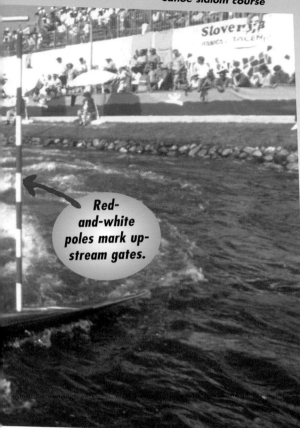

In the sprint events the water is flat and still, but in the slalom events canoeists must battle against a raging torrent!

Red-and-white poles mark up-stream gates.

SPLASHING OUT

Water rushes down the 300-metres long slalom course creating swirling whirlpools and powerful currents. Along the course are 25 'gates' which competitors must pass through without touching. Six of the gates must be negotiated up-stream.

U DIG?

The U-shaped slalom course at the Beijing Olympics is completely man-made. Workers dug out a whopping 1.10 million cubic metres of earth to complete it!

SUPER STATS

The artificial slalom in Beijing can be easily adjusted to set the level of difficulty of the course.

KAYAK: SLALOM

Unlike sprint kayaks, the boats used in slalom events must not have rudders. Instead the competitors must steer by paddling.

All competitors in the slalom events must wear safety helmets.

Kayak slalom course

KEEPING A WATCHFUL EYE

Up to three judges watch each gate on the course to see if the competitors touch them as they go through. All decisions are based on what the judges see with the naked eye.

SUPER STATS

In 1987, a British canoeist performed 1,000 Eskimo rolls in just 34 minutes, setting a new world record!

ROLL OVER

The power of the water tumbling down the course is often enough to capsize the boats and turn them upside down. But competitors just stay inside their canoe and paddle underwater to turn the right way up again. This technique is known as an Eskimo roll.

There are events for both men and women in the kayak slalom.

Life jackets are essential in all slalom events.

Competitors in the slalom events wear a 'spray deck' round their middle. This stretches across the top of the cockpit and makes it watertight.

The hole in which the competitor sits is called the cockpit.

Stepanka Hilgertova, Atlanta 1996

DID YOU KNOW?

Before the 1972 Olympics, the East German team spent months practising on an exact replica of the artificial river which had been built for the Games. They went on to win all the Gold medals!

The layout of the gates is redesigned for the final of each event.

Competitors from over 30 different countries will take part in the slalom events at the Games.

PUMP IT UP

Because Beijing's slalom course is not a natural flowing river, powerful pumps are needed to push the water at the bottom of the course back up to the top again. These pumps will have to work really hard as water cascades down the course at a rate of over 14 tonnes every second!

INDEX

A

49-er 3, 8, 9
470 8
Ainslie, Ben 6, 7
Alupei, Angela 17
Argentina 15
Athens 3
Atlanta (1996) 11-13, 15, 27, 28, 31
Australia 2, 11, 15, 20
Austria 14

B

Barcelona 19
Barton, Greg 24, 25
Beijing (2008) 11, 13, 14, 29, 31
Bekatorou, Sofia 9
Brazil 10, 15
Burcica, Constantina 17
Burnham, Kevin 8

C

Cal, David 22
canoes 22, 23, 26, 28, 29
catamarans 14, 15
Coope 20
Coubertin, Pierre de 3
coxless races 20, 21
coxswains 18, 19
Cracknell 20

D

Damian, Georgeta 21
Davies, Grant 24
Denmark 21
Dittmer, Andreas 23
Doktor, Martin 22, 23
double-handed dinghies 3, 8, 9, 10, 11

E

Egyptians 2
Eights 18
Elvström, Paul 3, 15
Elvström, Trine 15
Eskimo rolls 30
Estanguet, Tony 28
Europe 6, 7
Evers, Caroline 17
Evers, Georgina 17

F

Fernandez, Xavier 10
Ferreira, Marcelo 11
finn 6, 7, 11
Flach, Thomas 12
fleet races 8
Foernster, Paul 8
France 2, 13
Fredriksson, Gert 25
Fridman, Gal 4

G

Germany 12-13, 16-17, 22, 27
Gille, Christian 23
Ginn, Drew 20
Grael, Torben 11
Great Britain 2, 11, 13
Greece 2

H

Hagara, Roman 15
Hardy, Adrien 16
hiking out 7, 8
Hilgertova, Stepanka 31
Hochschorner, Pavel 29
Hochschorner, Peter 29
Hungary 22, 26

I

Ivanov, Vyacheslav 16, 17

J

Jaekel, Bernd 12
Janics, Natasa 25

K

Kaliska, Elena 31
kayaks 22, 24-7, 30-1
Knowles, Durward 11
Koeverden, Adam van 24
Kovacs, Katalin 25
Kucharski, Tomasz 16

L

Larsen, Eirik Veraas 24
laser 7
Lee Lai-shan 5
Lemieux, Lawrence 7
Lugbill, Jon 28

M

MacGregor, John 25
Martikan, Michal 28
Martinez, Iker 10
Meng, Guanliang 23
Merret, Faustine 5
mistral (see also RS:X) 4, 5
monotypes 7

N

Netherlands 18
Nilsson, Henrik 24
Norway 13

O

Olympic Games
  ancient 3
  1896 2, 3
  1900 2, 12, 19
  1924 11
  1932 11
  1936 25
  1948 3, 11, 15, 25
  1956 16
  1960 25
  1964 27
  1972 31
  1980 20
  1984 27
  1988 3, 11, 15, 24
  1992 19, 20, 28
  1996 11-13, 15, 23, 26-8, 31
  2000 3, 7, 9, 14, 29, 31
  symbol 3
  2004 4, 5, 6, 9, 10, 11, 17, 20
  2008 11, 13, 14, 29, 31
Oscarsson, Markus 24

P

Peschier, Benoit 30

R

Rauhe, Ronald 24
Romania 19
Rossi, Antonio 24, 25
rowing 2
RS: X (event formerly called mistral) 4, 5
Russia 13
Rutschow, Katrin 17

S

sailboarding 4, 5
sailing 3, 7
Scheidt, Robert 7
Schumann, Jochen 12
sculling 16, 17
single-handed sailing 6, 7
slalom 28, 29, 30, 31
soling 12, 13
Soviet Union 22
Spain 14
sprint races 22, 23, 24
star 10, 11, 12
Steinacher, Hans Peter 15
Susanu, Viorica 21
Sweden 11, 22
sweep oar 18, 19, 20, 21
Switzerland 2
Sycz, Robert 16
Sydney (2004) 3, 7, 9, 14-15, 29, 31

T

tacking 6, 7
Tomkins, James 20
tornado 14, 15
trapeze 8
trimarans 15
Tsoulfa, Aimilia 9
Tufte, Olaf 16

U

USA 13, 15, 18

V

Vandernotte, Noël 19
Vieilledent, Sebastien 16

W

Wieskoetter, Tim 24
Wylenzek, Tomasz 23

Y

Yang, Wenjun 23

Acknowledgements

We would like to thank Ian Hodge, Rosalind Beckman, Ben Hubbard and Elizabeth Wiggans for their assistance.
Cartoons by John Alston.
Copyright © 2000 ticktock Entertainment Ltd.
Revised edition 2008 ticktock Media Ltd., 2 Orchard Business Centre, North Farm Road, Tunbridge Wells, TN2 3XF, UK.

ISBN 978 1 84696 727 6

Picture Credits: t =top, b =bottom, c =centre, l =left, r =right, OFC =outside front cover, OBC =outside back cover, IFC =inside front cover

Ingrid Abery/ Action Plus: 12/13c. Allsport: IFC, 3br, 4t, 4/5 (main pic), 7tr, 11tr, 18/19c, 19bl, 20/21 (main pic), 25t, 26/27 (main pic), 27tr, 28/29 (main pic), 30t. Cancan Chu/ Getty Images: 14/15b. Empics: 16/17 (main pic), 17r, 22/23 (main pic), 24/25 (main pic), 28br, 30/31 (main pic). Evaristo SA/ AFP/ Getty Images: OFC. Kos Picture Source: 2/3 (main pic), 8/9 (main pic), 20/21b. Clive Mason/ Getty Images: 12b, 14/15t. PPL: 10/11 (main pic), 22t. Sipa Press/ Rex Features: 8t. Jamie Squire/ Getty Images: 20t.

Picture research by Image Select. Printed in China.